CHEAP frills

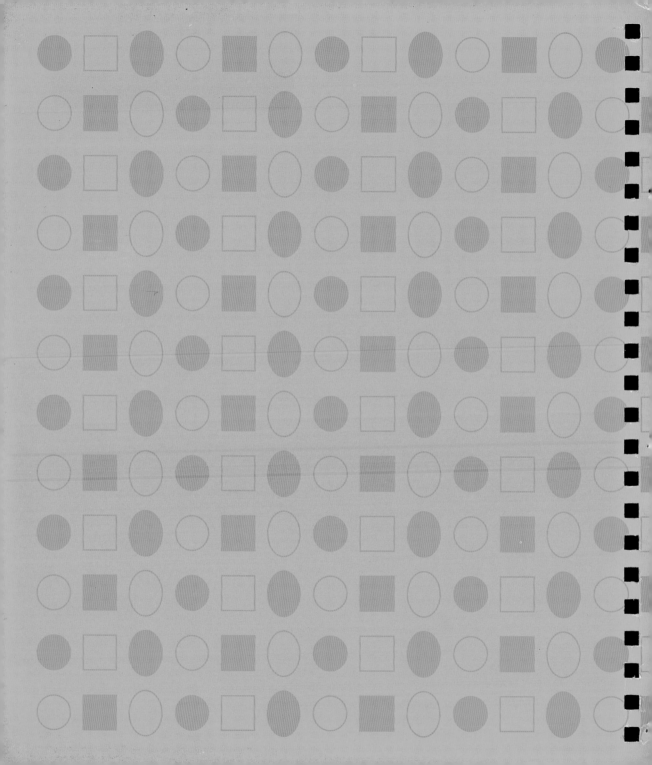

CHEAP frills

FABULOUS FACELIFTS FOR YOUR CLOTHES

BY *Jennifer Knapp*

PHOTOGRAPHY BY *David Magnusson*

ILLUSTRATIONS BY *Jennifer Knapp*

CHRONICLE BOOKS
SAN FRANCISCO

Library of Congress Cataloging-in-Publication Data available.

ISBN 0-8118-3019-5

Printed in China.

Book designed by CAROLE GOODMAN / BLUE ANCHOR DESIGN

Prop styling by Ethel Brennen

Distributed in Canada by Raincoast Books
9050 Shaughnessy Street
Vancouver, British Columbia V6P 6E5

10   9   8   7   6   5   4   3   2   1

Chronicle Books LLC
85 Second Street
San Francisco, California 94105

www.chroniclebooks.com

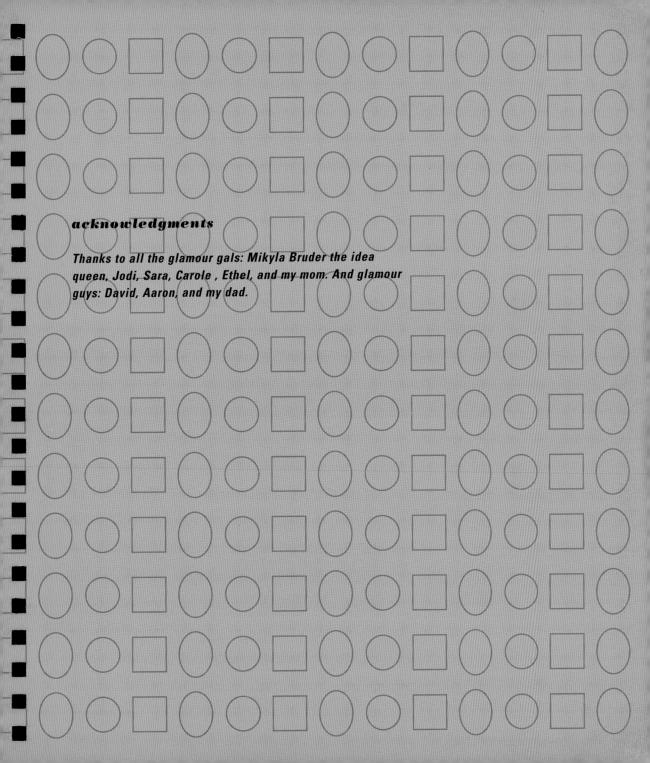

acknowledgments

Thanks to all the glamour gals: Mikyla Bruder the idea queen, Jodi, Sara, Carole , Ethel, and my mom. And glamour guys: David, Aaron, and my dad.

table of CONTENTS

introduction

Even if you make ritual offerings of big boxes of chocolate to the Goddess Audrey Hepburn, everybody, from comfy-sweater gal to glamour princess, has one thing in common: a shoe box (or Louis Vuitton trunk) full of embarrassing photos of unfortunate fashion choices. Mistakes will be made, so you might as well get out your wildest marabou boa and have fun with your wardrobe.

Relive your childhood days of dressing and undressing Barbies faster than you could crunch a Tootsie Pop. Remember? You would cut her long lamé skirt to a micro-mini, then make a bikini from a Jackie O suit, only to end up drawing a catsuit on her naked body with a magic marker.

Whether you're adorning a closet mainstay such as jeans or a cardigan, creating a luscious lace-front T-shirt, making a simple scarf, or revamping a too-worn-to-wear vintage find, the projects here should be a starting point for your imagination. Invent something dainty and demure (little do they know!) or outrageous and horn honking. You decide how far to take the details and the kooky colors.

There are plenty of perfectly good reasons to take on your closet. Maybe you're just bored with your yawn-inducing going-to-work clothes and you'd like to add a little zing. Have you been watching too many late movies and you long for the breezy style of your favorite fifties starlet buzzing around Capri on a Vespa? Maybe you can run down to the local mart for the crisp white shirt, but what about the flower-trimmed straw bag and that cute, cute scarf? Do you need a belly-dancing outfit to add a wacky wiggle to your day, or a hot tamale halter that's sexy in a chipped-nail-polish sort of way? Do you dream about the latest fad but there aren't enough pennies in the piggybank? Three words: *make it yourself!*

The big problem with revamping clothing seems to be our general horror of sewing. Along with ironing, dusting, and everything else we don't have time for, sewing has been swept up and dumped out the door of daily girly business. And, for the most part, good riddance! In school, we girls were likely to learn to change a tire and wire an electrical circuit while heating spaghetti with our free hand. Now we've grown up to be tough, in-control, cool girls who can order takeout and fix the plumbing if we feel like it. But alas, we can't sew beyond replacing a missing button. Well, that's all the skill that's needed for adorning clothes! For any stitches you need

to brush up on see Techniques (page 10). Or better yet, find a sewing machine at your local thrift store and make it do the work for you. We're not guys—we can read instructions (except stupid ones like those in the VCR manual). See Tools (page 110) for other items that will make any project a snap.

Finding the materials and trimmings is the creative part of any project. Look in fabric stores, thrifts, your best friend's closet, and your grandmother's sewing basket. You're more likely to find one-of-a-kind items and unique vintage pieces if you're willing to do a little digging (see Sources for more ideas, page 112).

Combining colors and textures is the most important part of revamping clothing. Are you as cool as a cherry popsicle or as hot as a cinnamon stick? See Materials (page 109) and Techniques (pages 10) for tips on creating a unique garment. Even the most hopelessly inartistic of us have some inner flair—or can copy at least!

Embrace fashion or ignore it. We can't be naked all the time, so glam it up and have fun. And owning a sewing machine won't wreck your devil-doll image (no one even has to know!). Just remember the unavoidable fact of fashion: No matter how fabulous your outfit, it's your glamorous guts that count. Razzle-dazzle them with your inner Superstar!

no-trouble TECHNIQUES

HAND STITCHING

Learning just a couple of stitches will get you on your way to adding trim, changing a hem, or fixing a seam. For decorative detail, try these stitches—big, chunky, and visible—using embroidery thread.

✳ *running stitch*

This is the granddaddy of all sewing stitches. If you learned to sew doing kindergarten projects, this is probably the stitch you used. The classic technique: Thread needle and knot one end of the thread. Guide the needle through the top of the fabric from the bottom, then back through the top to the bottom. Continue until you have a lovely dotted line of stitches. Make the stitches about ¼ inch long and ¼ inch apart. If you're ever at a loss about which stitch is the right one, use this basic stitch.

✳ *whipstitch*

This stitch runs along the edge of the fabric and binds it. Push a threaded needle up through the bottom of the fabric to the top, then around the edge and back to the bottom. Then up through the fabric to the top again, and around the edge, and through the fabric to the top. Continue until you finish binding the edge with this simple loop stitch. Space your stitches very close together to seal the raw edge of the fabric. This is the perfect stitch for attaching trimmings such as ribbon, and it is a good stitch to use for a buttonhole, too. Tiny, closely spaced whipstitches will be nearly invisible if you match the color of the thread to that of the fabric.

✳ *folk-art stitch*

This simple decorative stitch, a variation on the whipstitch, is also known as a blanket stitch. Begin by making one whipstitch. Now pull the needle through the loop along the edge. Begin another whipstitch ¼ inch from the first, and finish it off by pulling the needle and thread tightly through the loop. In this way, you will create a row of connected stitches. This is a good stitch to use on knit edges such as sweater necks, and around the edges of blanket and fleece garments.

✳ *hemming stitch*

A combo of the whipstitch and the running stitch, this invisible stitch is perfect for hemming. But you can use it wherever you want to hide your stitching. Fold the hem under and make a small perpendicular whipstitch between the hem edge and the main body of fabric. Then, slip the needle back under the stitch and make another whipstitch ½ inch to 1 inch away.

✳ *embroidery*

This is an art all its own, with hundreds of stitches (see Resources, page 113). A simple running stitch of bright embroidery thread is an easy trim for any garment. Once you've mastered that, try a cross-stitch.

SEWING TIPS

*inset seams

To allow space for threading a drawstring or creating button holes, inset the seam. Fold the raw edge of fabric under ½ inch, and ½ inch again, then sew along the fold, ½ inch in from the outer edge.

*seam allowance

When measuring and cutting fabric, remember to include a seam allowance. When cutting fabric that will be joined in a seam, add an inch or more to your measurements to account for the extra fabric needed to make the seam.

*sewing machines

Many people are terrified of these simple machines, yet they can speed up any project. And making a small investment in an old model doesn't mean you need to become a seamstress! Look for an old metal machine that sews a basic stitch. They are inexpensive, and a tune-up will have it working smoothly. There is nothing more satisfying than sewing a seam in a few minutes rather than a few hours.

*a note on patterns

This book presents diagrams and ideas, but you are responsible for making (or buying) any simple patterns that are necessary. Don't panic, it's easy! The easiest approach is to go to a fabric store and buy a pattern. Keep an eye out for Simplicity's New Look line of patterns: They're simple, inexpensive, and fashiony, too! Vintage patterns for classic styles may be found at thrift stores (just make sure that none of the pieces are missing). You can also make your own pattern by tracing the shape of an existing piece of clothing onto craft paper (leave a border for seam allowance), then cutting it out.

ADDING TRIMMING

✳ *ribbons*

Be fancy and create decorative loops and patterns with your ribbon. The easiest way to do this is to first draw a design on a piece of paper. Then, using regular ribbon or the kind with encased wires, loop, twist, or fold your ribbon into shape, pinning it in place on the paper pattern as you go. Iron the ribbon, then unpin it from the paper and carefully pin in place on the fabric. Using a running stitch or whipstitch, sew through the center of the ribbon and across any overlaps or folds.

✳ *beads*

You can use shiny, colorful beads to create all kinds of fun effects on fabric. Attach beads using beading thread and a beading needle (available at bead and fabric stores). Pull the single-threaded needle through the fabric from below, slip the bead onto the thread (you may have to unthread the needle temporarily for very small beads), and then pull the needle back through the fabric. It will look like a running stitch with a bead in the middle. To create designs with beads, first draw a pattern in tailor's chalk or a washable fabric pen on the garment. If you are not artistically inclined, use a photocopy of the pattern and use tracing paper and a tracing wheel (available at fabric stores) to transfer the design. Sew the beads along the transferred outline. Or, on printed fabric, simply sew beads along the lines of the pattern itself.

Use seed beads in various shapes to create different effects (see Resources, page 113). Make no mistake, this is a time-consuming process. To save time, look for ready-made beaded panels and fringe at fabric stores—some are not too outrageous but they are expensive. Or sew whole strands of beads to the garment: pin the strand in place and whipstitch it to the fabric. To create your own bead fringe, loop strands of beads off the hem. Make a stitch around the strand once every inch and let a 1½-inch loop dangle off the edge of the fabric.

✳ *sequins*

No time for beading? Use sequin ribbon instead. Pin the ribbon in
place and sew it to the fabric using a running stitch through the
center hole of each sequin. Or, to sew individual sequins to
fabric, pull the needle and thread, up through the fabric
and the center hole of the sequin, slip a bead onto the
thread and then push the needle back down through
the center hole. Sequins come in various shapes:
circles, squares, flowers, and even large mermaid scales.
Try them all.

CREATING FANCY SHAPES

Use fabric silhouettes to adorn all sorts of clothing items. Find images you like in
books, magazines, or coloring books. Photocopy your images, reducing or enlarging to
the desired size. Cut around the outline with scissors. Pin the photocopy to a piece
of fabric, such as felt, and cut the shape out with scissors; use a utility knife for any
details or interior cuts.

FITTING VINTAGE FINDS

There are some quick ways to refit vintage clothing without performing major surgery.
See Femme Fatale Laced-Back Sweater (page 48), and Ramona's Ribbon Sweater
(page 45), for some ideas. Be sure of what you have and what you're doing—do not
just cut up beautiful, irreplaceable vintage items. Opt for moving a button before
picking up scissors.

TIME-SAVING TRICKS

When you want a quick change—a few ribbons here, a simple ruffle there—try fabric
glue and fusible bindings, available at fabric stores. If you have an iron or enough time
to let the glue dry, these are easy fixes. However, they are not as permanent as sewing.

DYEING FABRIC

A bright wash of color instantly changes the look of any garment. Try dyeing jeans, T-shirts, and other natural-fiber clothing with liquid dye, available at any super-market. The liquids are best because they are less messy than the powders. But do not be fooled by their easy availability: dyes are dangerous and should not be touched or inhaled. Try searching on the Internet for companies specializing in dyes of bright and unusual colors. Remember that the color of the garment will affect the outcome of the dye job; for instance, pink dye on blue jeans will be purplish.

For fun, try this recipe for Kool-Aid dye. It works best on wool garments, but you can try it on other natural fibers for subtle tints. (Be aware, though, that some shrinkage might occur, so don't use it on your favorite wool sweater.) Mix together in a large pot 2 quarts water, 1 packet Kool-Aid powdered drink mix, $\frac{1}{3}$ cup vinegar, and 2 teaspoons salt. Immerse the fabric in the mixture and simmer at 180° F for 20 minutes. Wash the garment by hand with mild liquid soap or shampoo in cool water, rinse, and dry flat.

ADDING COLOR AND STYLE

The projects in this book are meant to spark your imagination. Use the colors and materials that are right for you and that fit your unique style. A combination of dark colors or subtle variations of one color will have a different effect than will a palette of bright, contrasting colors. If you are starting with a blue sweater, for instance, various shades of blue trim will be subtle and elegant, whereas bright orange trim will create a fun, over-the-top effect. For a look that's somewhere in between, decorate that blue sweater with a cobalt blue ribbon, light-blue beads, and a thin line of bright orange embroidery.

The same ideas apply to materials. A sweater trimmed with a pink velvet ribbon will have a very different look from one adorned with long pink fur. Before starting a project, lay out all the materials and look at various combinations of color and texture. Always take the garment with you as you go about finding trimmings for it. If you feel overwhelmed by the task of selecting colors, look through magazines for combos that you like. There are also many design books available on vintage style, color schemes, and the use of fabrics and trimmings—look for them in the library.

girly-gang t-shirts and betty blouses

Grab your best gal pals and try making some of these vampy vixen tees, spicy tops, and halters. Start with tees you have, or look for inexpensive strappy tees in the little girls' section—these are available in a surprising range of sizes. No one can have too many temptress tops.

Go-Go Party T-Shirt (page 21)

red hot sophia loren T-SHIRT

Need to tell someone off in fiery style and still have him worship the ground you stomp on? Here's half the outfit. This spitfire Italian peasant tee will make you want to throw some plates.

Scissors
1 short-sleeved, slightly baggy T-shirt
Iron
Pins

Needle or a sewing machine
Thread to match the T-shirt
1 safety pin
1 yard ¼-inch-wide ribbon or cord
1½ feet ¼-inch-wide elastic

1 Using scissors, cut out a big scoop neck on the T-shirt, front and back, from the top of one sleeve to the other.

2 Fold the raw edge under ½ inch, and press with the iron. Fold under ½ inch again, and press. Pin to secure.

3 Using the needle and thread or a sewing machine, sew an inset seam (see page 12) along the fold, almost ½ inch from the outer edge, with a running stitch (see page 10). This will create a channel for the ribbon. Remove pins.

4 Make two small slits ½ inch apart in the center front of the neck channel. Snip through only the outer layer of fabric.

5 Fold the sleeves under ½ inch, and press. Pin to secure. Using a running stitch, sew an inset seam ½ inch from

the outer edge almost all the way around, leaving a ½ inch opening at the back of the T-shirt. Remove pins.

6 Attach the safety pin to one end of the ribbon and, using the safety pin as a guide, thread the ribbon into one of the openings in the neck channel, and out the other hole. Remove the safety pin. Tie the ribbon ends into a bow in the front.

7 Cut the elastic into two 9-inch lengths. Attach the safety pin to the end of one piece and thread the elastic into the sleeve opening, through the channel, and out again. Remove the safety pin. Tightly knot the elastic ends or stitch together, to create a puffed sleeve. Repeat on the other sleeve.

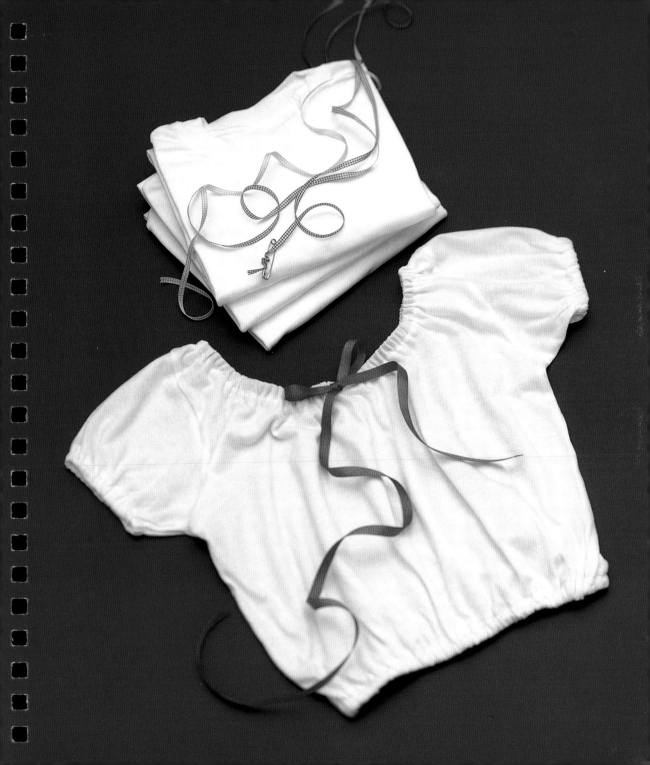

brigitte bardot ribbon T-SHIRT

Ooh la la! Pair this charming tie-at-the-shoulders tee with a little scarf around your neck and you're Brigitte B. on a picnic. All you need is some stinky cheese and a bottle of wine!

Scissors
1 camisole-style T-shirt
Tape measure
3½ yards velvet ribbon ¼ inch wide
Pins
Needle or a sewing machine
Thread to match the ribbon
Optional: beads or other trim

1 Using scissors, cut the straps off the T-shirt.

2 Using the tape measure, determine the ribbon lengths needed for your T-shirt (see illustration). You'll need four lengths: two short lengths (about 8 inches each) to go across the front and the back of the neck and two longer lengths (about 44 inches each) to go under the arms and up to tie at the top of the shoulders. Cut the ribbon according to your measurements.

3 Pin the two shorter lengths of ribbon horizontally to the front and the back of the T-shirt neck. Using the needle and thread or a sewing machine, sew along both edges of the ribbons with a running stitch or a whipstitch (see page 10).

4 Fold one of the longer lengths of ribbon in half so that the ends meet. Pin the ribbon at its midpoint to the top of the side seam under the arm. Pin the ribbon around one of the arm openings until it meets up with the neck and back ribbons. Using a running stitch or whipstitch, sew in place along both edges of the ribbon. Repeat on the other side. Remove all pins.

5 Try the T-shirt on and tie the ribbons at the shoulders for a perfect fit. Trim off excess ribbon.

6 If desired, sew beads or other trim, such as braiding, bead fringe, or embroidered ribbon, along the bottom hem of the T-shirt.

go-go party T-SHIRT

As colorful as a candy neck-lace, this confetti party tee covered with festive ribbons will make you want to jump on the bed. Look in a craft store for a rhinestone attach-ment tool to add a gaudy twinkle. For a flowery feel, see the variation below.

Scissors
12 yards ¼-inch-wide satin ribbon (twelve 1-yard lengths, each in a different color)
Fabric glue
1 camisole-style T-shirt
Needle
Thread to match the ribbon
Optional: Beads, rhinestone-attachment tool and mini-rhinestones

1 Using scissors, cut the ribbons into 1½-inch lengths.

2 Knot each piece of ribbon in the center and trim the ends to ½ inch.

3 After tying and trimming each ribbon, dip the ends in fabric glue to seal.

4 If desired, sew a bead to the center of each ribbon for an extra twinkle. Or, if you have a rhinestone-attachment tool, affix a rhinestone to each ribbon.

5 Cover the front and the straps of the shirt with the ribbon knots, using the needle and thread to sew them in place. Set the ribbon knots so close together that the entire shirt surface is covered and the fabric is not visible.

Variation: Instead of using ribbon knots, trim the tee with little silk flowers and sequins. Stitch them along the straps and clustered at the hem, then sew them in a pattern that looks as if the flowers are growing up the bodice. Stitch with embroidery thread around the flowers to create stems and leaves.

heidi T-SHIRT

Even if the hills are alive with the sound of sirens, you'll look as sweet as edel-weiss. Trim a strappy tee up the front and lace with ribbon, then add as much or as little detail as you wish.

Tape measure
1 camisole-style T-shirt
Pins
Scissors
Iron
Needle or a sewing machine
Thread to match the T-shirt
1½ yards ¼-inch-wide ribbon
Optional: Tiny fabric flowers, beads, embroidered ribbon, beaded fringe, rhinestones

1 Using the tape measure, determine the center of the T-shirt front, measuring from side seam to side seam. Mark it with a vertical line of pins, from neckline to bottom hem.

2 Using scissors, cut the T-shirt front in half, straight up the pin line. As you cut, remove each pin.

3 Fold each raw edge under ¼ inch, and press with the iron. Fold under ½ inch again, and press. Pin to secure.

4 Using the needle and thread or a sewing machine, sew an inset seam (see page 12) with a running stitch. This will create panels for the lacing. Remove pins.

5 Along the length of each panel, mark every 2 inches with pins.

6 At each pin, snip a ¼-inch horizontal opening through all layers of fabric. Remove pins.

7 Using a whipstitch (see page 10), carefully bind the edges of each hole.

8 Starting at the neck, crisscross the ribbon through the holes, like you are lacing a shoe. Tie a bow at the bottom.

9 If desired, add tiny flowers, beads, and embroidered ribbon around the neck, hem, and straps. Or add beaded fringe to the hem and rhinestones around the neck.

22

disco iron-on T-SHIRT

There are a few ways to make funky iron-ons. The easiest is to take an image to your neighborhood copy shop and have it color-copied onto iron-on paper. This is now available for the home computer as well.

If your T-shirt is a dark color (like the one pictured), iron transfer to white fabric first, then sew it to the T-shirt using a running stitch (see page 10).

If you'd like to discover your inner Frida Kahlo, try this crayon iron-on.

Crayons

1 piece of medium-grit sandpaper, approximately 8 inches by 10 inches

1 piece of cardboard, approximately 10 inches by 12 inches

1 T-shirt, previously washed

Iron

1 dishcloth

½ cup vinegar and 1 cup water, mixed in a bowl

Glitter nail polish

3 tablespoons salt and 1 quart water, mixed in a bowl

Optional: Ribbon, ball fringe, and sequin ribbon

1 Using crayons, draw a lovely picture on the gritty side of the sandpaper. Press fairly hard so that the color goes on thick and a lot of crayon wax gets on the sandpaper.

2 Lay the T-shirt flat and place the cardboard inside the shirt. Place the sandpaper, crayon side down, on the front of the T-shirt. Make sure the sandpaper and cardboard are aligned. Using the iron on a medium-hot to hot setting, press the sandpaper until the crayon melts into the fabric. Remove sandpaper.

3 Soak the dishcloth in the vinegar-and-water mixture. Wring out the cloth and lay it over the crayon design on the T-shirt. Iron on a hot setting to set the crayon. Remove the dishcloth.

4 Add a sparkle with dots of glitter nail polish. Let dry. Remove the cardboard.

5 Soak the T-shirt in the salt water for 3 hours to set the image.

6 Machine wash in warm water with mild soap and tumble-dry low.

7 If desired, add ribbon and ball fringe to the hem and sequin ribbon around the iron-on design.

show-off sweater halter

The most elegant halter ever! A great way to reuse a fave sweater that has seen better days. Use a fitted pullover that isn't too thick or too itchy; cashmeres, cottons, and soft synthetics are best.

Scissors
1 crewneck pullover sweater
Pins
Needle or a sewing machine
Thread to match the sweater
1 safety pin
1 yard silk cord or ¼-inch-wide velvet ribbon

1 Using scissors, cut off the arms of the sweater. Cut a straight line across the front just under the neck (see illustration). Trim off the back, beginning at the side seam just under one arm and trimming, as low as you dare, across to the other side seam (see illustration).

2 Around the back and under the arms, fold the fabric under ¼ inch, and then ¼ inch again. Pin to secure. Using the needle and thread or a sewing machine, sew the hem with a running stitch (see page 10).

3 Along the front neck, fold the edge under ½ inch. Fold under ½ inch again. Pin to secure. Using a running stitch, sew an inset seam (see page 12) along the fold, almost ½ inch from the outer edge. This will create a channel for the cord.

4 Attach the safety pin to one end of the cord and using the safety pin as a guide, thread the end of the cord through the channel and out the other side. Remove the safety pin. Knot the ends of the cord.

hotsy hankie HALTER

Our favorite trailer-park tops make you feel as cool as a creamsicle in summer, and look as hot as a new red lipstick. Look for a mod geometric or tacky travel scarf. This breeze of a hankie top is just barely there—so make sure no one grabs it after they sneeze.

20-inch-by-20-inch vintage hankie or scarf
Iron
Pins
Needle or a sewing machine
Thread to match the scarf
1 safety pin
3 yards silk cord
Scissors
Iron
Optional: Beads or
    sequin ribbon

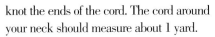

1 Fold one edge of the hankie under ½ inch, and press with the iron. Pin to secure. Using the needle and thread or a sewing machine, sew an inset seam (see page 12) along the fold, almost ½ inch from the outer edge, with a running stitch (see page 10). This will create a channel for the cord. Remove pins.

2 Attach the safety pin to one end of the silk cord and, using the safety pin as a guide, thread the end of the cord through the channel and out the other end. Remove the safety pin.

3 Put the cord around your neck and tie it in back, with the hankie hanging loose in front. Using scissors, trim one end of the cord to the proper length, center it in the channel, and

knot the ends of the cord. The cord around your neck should measure about 1 yard.

4 The hankie should fall to just below your waist. Trim off any excess fabric from the bottom edge. Fold the raw edge under ¼ inch, and press with the iron. Fold under ¼ inch again, and press. Using a hemming stitch (see page 11), sew the hem along the length.

5 Cut the remaining silk cord into four 1½-foot lengths. Sew one length on each side of the hankie at the bustline. Sew the other lengths, one on each side, just above the waistline (see illustration).

6 Try on the halter, tying all the cords in the back. Trim the cords to manageable lengths and knot the ends.

i-dream-of-genie TOP

Make this hot, belly-baring top and grant some wishes for yourselves, girls! Visit your local Indian-import shop to stock up on the necessary materials: beads, bindi dots (forehead dots), and a choli top (the short-sleeved garment worn under a sari; a snug-fitting, cropped T-shirt will also work).

Needle
Thread to match the *choli* top
1 *choli* top
1 yard ½-inch-wide ribbon
12 *bindi* dots
Two or three 12-inch-long strands of seed beads
Scissors
Multipurpose cement glue
Optional: 4 yards sequin ribbon, 24 mermaid scales (round disks with a hole on one edge, used mostly for costumes)

1 Using a running stitch (see page 10), sew one or two rows of ribbon around the hem.

2 If your seed bead strands are in loops, using scissors, cut each loop at the knot. Tie off both ends and seal each knot with a drop of multipurpose cement glue. Let the glue dry.

3 Sew a line of seed beads around the neckline by laying the strands end to end and taking a stitch every inch.

4 Add *bindi* dots around the neck, attaching them using a needle and thread.

5 If desired, sew the sequin ribbon in a swirling pattern over the bodice (see page 46), and add mermaid scales along the hem.

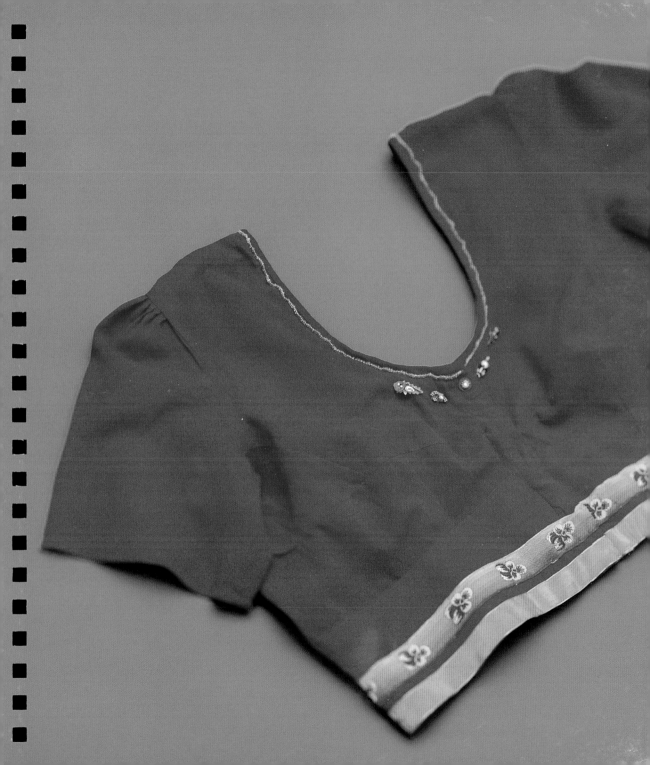

 capri T-SHIRT

The lovely isle of Capri is home to sunny beaches, Vespas, straw bags, and those infamous pants. Here's the perfect eyelet-lace-trimmed tee to go with your capris. You'll look as cool as gelato, even if you're sweating in your Dodge Dart.

1 sleeveless, fitted white T-shirt
Scissors
Iron
Needle or a sewing machine
White thread
Tape measure
White eyelet lace (see step 2 below
   to determine length)

1 The T-shirt should end at your waist; if it doesn't, using scissors, trim it to waist length. Fold the raw edge under ¼ inch, and press with the iron. Fold under ¼ inch again, and press. Using the needle and thread or a sewing machine, sew the hem with a running stitch or hemming stitch (see pages 10 and 11).

2 Using the tape measure, determine the width of the front of the T-shirt from one side seam to the other. Multiply this width by 8 to determine the amount of eyelet lace needed. Cut the lace into the 8 equal lengths.

3 Sew one length to the bottom of the front hem with a running stitch.

4 Sew the next length above the first, overlapping it by ⅛ inch. Continue up the front of the shirt with all 8 lengths. The last row of lace should be just below the bustline.

kiki's parisian boudoir T-SHIRT

Bonjour mon amour, kiss, kiss! Don't venture outside in this lace-trimmed tee or you'll be mobbed on the rue di Rivoli by a bunch of artists who haven't showered in weeks.

Tape measure
1 camisole-style T-shirt
Pins
Needle or a sewing machine
Thread to match the lace
1½ yards (non-synthetic stuff)
   ¼-inch-wide lace
Scissors
1 tiny silk flower
Optional: Beads

1 Using the tape measure, vertically divide the front of the T-shirt hem into five evenly spaced sections. Using pins, mark each measurement. Then pin a vertical ⅛-inch fold on the outside of the T-shirt at each mark, beginning at the hem and ending below the bustline. Using the needle and thread or a sewing machine, sew up each fold with a running stitch (see page 10).

2 Pin a strip of lace along the length of each shoulder strap. Using scissors, cut the lace to fit. Using a running stitch, sew the lace to the strap.

3 Pin another strip of lace diagonally to the front of the bodice, from the base of one strap to the opposite side seam (about 6 inches down from the top of the side

seam). Trim the excess lace at the side seam. Repeat on the other side, completing the cross-your-heart pattern. Sew the lace to the T-shirt.

4 Pin a length of lace horizontally across the front of the T-shirt below the bust-line. Sew the lace to the T-shirt.

5 Pin two lengths of lace to the tee between the base of the shoulder straps and the top of the side seams. Sew in place. Remove all pins.

6 Trim the T-shirt along the upper edge of the lace between the straps on the bodice, creating a V neck.

7 Sew the tiny flower to the spot where the lace crosses your heart. If desired, decorate the lace by sewing beads along the neckline and straps, or create a bead pattern on the bodice (see page 13).

cha-cha ruffle TOP

Add a simple ruffle to a long-sleeved top and you'll be ready for your cha-cha or rumba lesson. One, two, cha-cha-cha!

Tape measure
1 long-sleeved pullover top
Scissors
½ yard fabric (velvet, sheer, or satin)
Iron
Needle or a sewing machine
Thread to match the top
Pins

1 Using the tape measure, determine the circumference of the shirt hem. Using scissors, cut a strip of the fabric 2 inches wide by 1½ times the hem measurement. (You may need to join a few strips of fabric together to achieve this length.)

2 Fold one long side of the fabric under ¼ inch, and press with the iron. Fold under ¼ inch again, and press.

Using the needle and thread or a sewing machine, sew the hem with a running stitch (see page 10).

3 Create a ruffle by pinning the raw edge of the fabric to the inside of the shirt hem, gathering the fabric a bit as you go.

4 Sew the ruffle in place with a running stitch. Remove pins.

5 If you're pleased with your handiwork, use the leftover fabric to create a ruffle for the sleeve cuffs or for a skirt—to add an extra va-va-voom to your step.

tarty T-HALTER

A simple way to girlify an old T-shirt. This playful, center-tie tee is raced out with fast side stripes.

Tape measure
1 T-shirt
Pins
Washable fabric pen

Scissors
2 yards ½-inch-wide velvet or
    grosgrain ribbon
Needle or a sewing machine
Thread to match the velvet and
    the white or black ribbon
1 yard ½-inch-wide white or
    black grosgrain ribbon

1 Using the tape measure, determine the center point of the T-shirt front, measuring from side seam to side seam. Mark it with a pin just below the neck.

2 Using the tape measure and the washable fabric pen, draw a straight line from the center of the pin to the top of the side seam. Using scissors, cut along the marked line.

3 Repeat on the other side.

4 Cut a horizontal line straight across the back, from side seam to side seam, beginning at the end of your first front cut and trimming across to the other cut.

5 Fold the velvet ribbon in half to determine the midpoint of the ribbon length, and mark it with a pin. Determine the center point of the T-shirt back, measuring from side seam to side seam. Mark it with a pin. Pin the velvet ribbon along the raw edge, starting at the center back and moving under the arm and around the front to the top of the point. Repeat on the other side. The ribbons will cross at the top of the point. Using the needle and thread or a sewing machine, sew along both ribbon edges with a running stitch or a whipstitch (see page 10). Remove all pins.

6 Measure the length of the shirt along the side seam from under the arm to the bottom edge. Cut four lengths of the black or white grosgrain ribbon, each to that length. Pin the "racing stripes" in place, two along each side seam. Using a running stitch or a whipstitch along the edges of the ribbon, sew in place.

wild & wooly sweaters

Knit fabric can be scary to work with because it unravels but, contrary to logic, sweaters can be cut up and seamed just like other fabrics. There are plenty of hideous sweaters from earlier decades that are actually made from nice, natural yarns. If you don't like the color simply dye the garment before you start one of these projects—your sweater will thank you for your kindness, as will the world!

Snow Bunny Cardigan (page 40)

snow bunny CARDIGAN

You can create this zip-front cardigan in a jiffy. Before you know it, you'll be winning a snowball fight.

Scissors
1 cardigan
Pins
Needle or a
   sewing machine

Thread to match the cardigan
1 zipper, the length of your cardigan,
   faux sheepskin, and ribbon
Yarn
Large-eyed needle
Tape measure
$\frac{1}{2}$ yard fuzzy white faux sheepskin
2 yards $\frac{1}{4}$-inch-wide cotton ribbon

1 Using scissors, cut the buttons off of the cardigan. Fold under the button and button-hole panels and pin.

2 Using the needle and thread or a sewing machine, sew in the zipper with a running stitch (see page 10).

3 Using yarn and a large-eyed needle, sew a decorative running stitch or cross-stitch (see page 11) along each side of the zipper.

4 Using the tape measure, determine the circumferences of the sleeve cuffs, neck, and hem. Cut four pieces of faux sheep-skin 4 inches wide; cut two of these pieces to the length of the cuff circum-ference, one piece to the length of the neck circumference, and one piece to the length of the hem circumference.

5 Fold each piece of faux sheepskin in half lengthwise around the edge of the cuffs, neck, and hem. Pin in place. Using a running stitch or a whipstitch (see page 10), sew the sheepskin in place. Remove pins.

6 Cut two pieces of ribbon to the length of the sleeve cuff circumference, and one piece to the length of the hem circumfer-ence. Using a running stitch, sew the ribbon in a line just above the fur on the cuffs and hem.

Variation: Find a hood pattern and cut it out of knit or fleece. Instead of the faux sheepskin, attach the hood to the neckline. Then sew the faux fur to the outside edge of the hood, so the fur frames your face.

fabulous fur CARDIGAN

Is that scream-at-the-top-of-your-lungs Vegas-showgirl dazzle missing from your life, not to mention your wardrobe? Fix that problem now! A few sequins will do the trick.

1 cardigan
Scissors
Pins
Needle or a sewing machine
Thread to match the cardigan
Tape measure
½ yard faux fur
2 yards sequin ribbon
Sequins
Beads
Fabric flowers
Embroidery thread
Glitzy buttons (one for each buttonhole)

1 The cardigan should end at your waist; if it doesn't, using scissors, trim it to waist length. Fold the edge under ½ inch, and pin. Using the needle and thread or a sewing machine, sew the hem with a running stitch or a hemming stitch (see pages 10 and 11).

2 Using the tape measure, measure 9 inches up from the hem at the center front of the sweater, and mark it with a pin. Using the tape measure and pins as a guide, cut a straight line from this mark up to the shoulder seam at the neckline. Repeat on the other side to create a V neck. If necessary, trim the back of the neckline to adjust for the changes in front.

3 Cut the fur into a shawl collar (see illustration), adjusting to fit your particular cardigan.

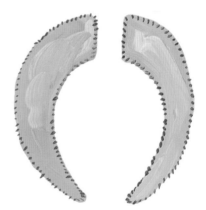

(continued)

4 Fold the outer edges of the collar under ¼ inch. Using a whipstitch (see page 10), hem the folded edge.

5 Pin the collar in place around the neck. Using a running stitch or whipstitch, sew the collar onto the cardigan. When the collar is folded flat, the seam should be invisible beneath it.

6 Now add decoration. Using a running stitch, sew a line of sequin ribbon 1½ inches above the bottom hem and above the hem of each cuff. Or sew looping lines of sequin ribbon up the front from the hem. Dot sequins across the sleeves and body of the cardigan, attaching each sequin with needle and thread, securing it with a bead in the center (see page 13). Stitch fabric flowers clustered along the hem. Stitch the embroidery thread around the flowers to create stems and leaves.

7 If desired, replace the buttons with glitzy, show-stopping ones.

Variation: Instead of making a faux fur collar, simply sew a marabou boa around the neck.

fifties beaded CARDIGAN REVISITED

Fifties cardigans, all covered with beads and sequins, are so sweet, but they cost a fortune! This project puts you on the fast track to a fifties look. Find a rhinestone-attachment tool at a craft-supply store. You'll be revving up your hot rod in no time.

Scissors
½ yard flashy, colorful vinyl, or velvet
  for a fancier look
Rhinestone-attachment tool
Mini-rhinestones
1 cardigan
Optional: Needle, thread, sequins, and beads

1 Using scissors, cut a bunch of shapes out of the vinyl. Try flower shapes, from mod daisies to simple tulips. Or how about a bad-girl hot-rod motif: candy-apple-red cars, low-rider flames, rear-view-mirror dice, and mud-flap girls? (See page 14 for more on creating perfect cutouts.)

2 Using a rhinestone-attachment tool and mini-rhinestones—or needle and thread and sequins and beads—attach each cutout to the cardigan.

ramona's ribbon SWEATER

As simple as a bat of the eyelashes, a single ribbon can become a charming detail when woven through a loose-knit sweater. If you can't find a loose-knit or crocheted pullover, see the variations below.

1 loose-knit pullover
1 to 2 yards ½-inch-wide grosgrain ribbon
Fabric glue

1 Beginning at the center front of the sweater just below the bustline, weave the ribbon in and out of the knit in a horizontal line, at 1-inch intervals. Continue weaving around the whole sweater, ending at the center front, where you started.

2 Tie a bow in the front, trimming the ribbon ends short and sealing them with a dab of fabric glue on each edge.

Variation 1: If your pullover is tightly knit, snip ⅛-inch holes in the sweater just below the bustline, at 1-inch intervals. Using a whipstitch (see page 10) and matching thread, bind the edges of the holes. Weave the ribbon through the holes and tie in the front.

Variation 2: If you can't bear to cut holes in your tightly knit sweater but you'd like to add a ribbon detail, try this: From just below the bust, starting at each side seam, measure and mark the point halfway to center front. Make a small ½-inch-long, ⅛-inch-deep vertical fold on each mark and insert a 6-inch length of ribbon on each side. Sew through the folds and ribbons with a couple stitches in a matching thread. Tie the ribbons together in front.

frumpy to fab CARDIGAN

*Old, baggy grandpa cardigans
are nice and warm, but please,
ma chéri . . . trim a bit here and
add a bit there, for one that's
cute and comfy. Voilá!*

Scissors
1 cardigan
Pins

Needle or a sewing machine
Thread to match the cardigan
Tape measure
½ yard sheer fabric
Iron
3 yards ½-inch-wide velvet ribbon
1½ yards bead-embroidered ribbon

1 Using scissors, trim the cardigan to waist length. Fold the raw edge under ½ inch, then ½ inch again. Pin to secure. Using needle and thread or a sewing machine, sew the hem with a running stitch or a hemming stitch (see pages 10 and 11).

2 Cut the buttons off the cardigan. Fold under the button and buttonhole panels, and pin. Using a vertical running stitch, sew both folds in place.

3 Using a tape measure, determine the circumference of the hem. Cut a piece of sheer fabric 2 inches wide and the length of the hem measurement. Fold one of the long edges and both the short ends of the sheer fabric under ¼ inch, and press with the iron. Fold under ¼ inch again, and press. Using a running stitch, sew the hem.

4 Pin the raw edge of the fabric to the outside edge of the cardigan hem. Using a running stitch, sew the fabric in place. Remove pins.

5 Using a running stitch or a whipstitch (see page 10), sew the velvet ribbon to the cardigan, covering the raw edge, and around each cuff. Using a running stitch, sew the bead-embroidered ribbon along the top edge of the velvet ribbon.

6 Cut four 6-inch lengths of velvet ribbon. Sew one to each side of the front, at the neck and bustline, to create the closures.

Variation: Add a flourish with a swirling ribbon design. The best ribbon to use is the ¼-inch kind with encased wire on one edge. Draw a pattern on paper first. Pin the ribbon along the pattern. Using an iron on a medium setting, press the ribbon. Using a running stitch, sew right down the middle of the ribbon, following the loops and curls, to attach it.

femme fatale laced-back SWEATER

A tiny but tantalizing twist for the back of a sweater, shirt, or even a dress. This is an easy way to fit a vintage item without a trip to the tailor.

Scissors
1 foot silk cord
Tape measure
1 cardigan
Pins
Tailor's chalk
Iron
Needle or a sewing machine
Thread to match the sweater
2 yards ¼-inch-wide ribbon

1 Using scissors, cut eight 1½ -inch lengths of silk cord. Set aside.

2 Using a tape measure, determine the width of the sweater back, from side seam to side seam. Divide the width into quarters, marking each section with a pin.

3 Using the tailor's chalk, draw two vertical lines up the back of the sweater, from the sweater bottom hem to the shoulders, at the two outside pin marks (see illustration). Remove pins.

4 Beginning 3 inches from the sweater bottom, make four chalk dots, 1½ inches apart, along each vertical line.

5 Pin a ⅛-inch fold along the vertical lines. Pin a loop of your pre-cut silk cord into the fold at each dot, and press with an iron.

6 Using the needle and thread or a sewing machine, sew a running stitch (see page 10) along each fold (see illustration). Remove pins and press.

7 Lace the ribbon through the loops in a crisscross pattern and tie a bow at the bottom.

48

sad sweater FIRST-AID

Vintage sweaters are easy to find and fun to wear. However, many have been snacked on by pesky insects or suffered other wear and tear, leaving them sad and ratty. Give an old sweater a happy new life with a few well-placed trimmings.

Pins
2 yards flower-chain trim
1 seen-better-days sweater
Scissors
Needle or a sewing machine
Thread to match the ribbon
2 yards 1-inch-wide velvet ribbon
Sequins, beads, and other trimmings

1 Pin a length of flower-chain trim around the bottom edge of the sweater. Using scissors, trim off any excess. Using the needle and thread or a sewing machine, sew it in place with a running stitch (see page 10).

2 Pin lengths of velvet ribbon around the collar, hem, and cuffs. Trim off any excess. Using a running stitch or whipstitch (see page 10), sew along both edges of the velvet ribbons to attach them.

3 Continue to add rows of trim until all the major holes and damage are covered.

4 Dot sequins all over the body and sleeves, making sure to cover any remaining small holes. Attach each sequin individually, securing it with a bead in the center (see page 13).

pinch-my-bottoms & swinging skirts

One of the fun things about being girls is that we can wear skirts whenever we feel like it! Nothing shows off your glam gams better. Here are some ideas for dressing up skirts you already have, and one for creating a simple do-it-yourself wrap skirt. But first, a couple of comfy bottoms for going out, and staying in.

Pippi's Out-on-the-Town Skirt (page 62)

the not-so-BASIC BLUE

Jeans have been abused through-out the ages—from hippie patches to disco studs. People just can't seem to leave them in their simple, blue peace. And for good reason! Jeans are the perfect place to practice your decora-tive skills. Everyone has an old pair languishing in the closet. Whether you want to make a retro statement, a unique expres-sion, or just have fun, you can't go wrong with jeans. Experiment with stitches, colors, and fabric combos. Test out dyeing by trying an over-dye (see page 15). Make your jeans an ongoing project. And, don't forget—denim skirts, capris, and jackets can be trimmed in a similar way.

Scissors
Colorful fabrics from around
   the world, thrift finds, and vintage
   material
1 pair of jeans
Pins
2 to 6 yards ribbon (satin, lace, or
   any other patterns you fancy)
Needle
Thread to match the colorful fabrics
3 or 4 skeins embroidery thread
Embroidery needle
Optional: Miniature silk flowers, mermaid
   scales, laminated photos, sequins, flowers, faux fur, iron-ons, patches, glittery
   fabric paint, and bead fringe

1 Using scissors, cut the fabric into strips of various widths.

2 Starting at the bottom of the jeans legs, pin rows of fabric strips and ribbon to the jeans. Using a needle and thread, sew a running stitch (see page 10) along the edges of each row of trim. Remove pins.

3 Using embroidery thread and the embroidery needle, sew a dotted line or something fancy (see page 11) above the ribbon and fabric trim.

4 Add a row of miniature rosebuds, or another trim of your choice.

5 Keep adding rows until you're happy with the look. Or go crazy and cover the entire surface of the jeans with mermaid scales, flowers, little laminated photographs, sequins, fur, iron-ons, patches, glittery fabric paint, and beaded fringe.

pj's for DAY

Inexpensive Chinese pajama bottoms feel just like a butterfly kiss—you'll want to wear them all the time. And why not? Crop them to make capris, trim them to create pedal pushers, or put a jingle in them with these harem pants.

2 or 3 strands of seed beads
Scissors
Multipurpose cement glue
Chinese pajama bottoms
Needle
Thread to match the pajama bottoms
24 mermaid scales
12 bells
Pins
1 foot ¼-inch-wide elastic
1 safety pin

1 If your seed bead strands are in loops, using scissors, cut the loop at the knot. Tie off both ends and seal each knot with a drop of multipurpose cement glue. Let the glue dry.

2 Lay the strands of seed beads end to end just below the waistband of the pajama bottoms. Using needle and thread, sew a stitch every inch, letting a 1½-inch length of beads dangle between each stitch (see page 13).

3 Sew on a row of mermaid scales, evenly spaced, just above the beads.

4 Sew a bell to every second scale.

5 Fold the hem of each leg under ½ inch. Pin in place. Using a running stitch (see page 10), sew almost all the way around each hem, leaving a ½-inch opening at the inseam.

6 Cut the elastic into two 6-inch lengths. Attach the safety pin to one length and, using the safety pin as a guide, thread the elastic through the opening in one of the leg hems, around the hem, and out again. Tightly knot or stitch together the two ends of elastic so that the fabric gathers at the hem (but not so tight that it pinches your ankle). Trim off any excess elastic and stitch the opening closed. Repeat on the other leg.

simplest skirt ever: THE WRAP

Mod sixties prints, fifties aprons, pony blankets, sheer slips, and sari silks all look fantastic in this wrap-around-your-waist style. Make one for every day of the week, or, better yet, one for every mood. See the variation below for a slinky ribbon wrap style for long skirts.

1 wrap-skirt pattern
1½ to 2 yards fabric (vintage prints, faux fur, blanket, fleece, leather, try anything!)
Tape measure
Scissors
Pins
Iron
Needle or a sewing machine
Thread to match fabric
2 yards ½-inch-wide ribbon
Optional: Bead fringe, lace, ribbon, a marabou boa, 2 Velcro dots

1 Check out your local fabric store for a simple wrap-skirt pattern. Or, if you dare, move right along to step 2 and wing it.

2 Wrap the fabric around your waist and use the tape measure to find the width required. Then, add on enough of an overlap in front—at least 1 foot—so that you're not showing your skivvies, darling! Using scissors, cut the fabric to the width you need and the length you desire, whether it be long and flowing or micro-mini.

3 Wrap the fabric around your waist, inside out, and pin together at the waist. You will need to create darts so the fabric flows smoothly over your hips (see illus-

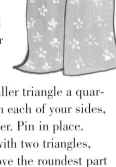

tration): Pinch together one triangle of fabric at each of your sides above your hip bone (the larger end of the triangle will be up at your waist, and the point will be over your hips). Pin the dart in place. Then pinch together a smaller triangle a quarter of the way in from each of your sides, toward the front center. Pin in place. Repeat in the back with two triangles, one on each side above the roundest part of your bottom. The fabric should now flow over your curves without being tight.

(continued)

4 Take off the fabric. Fold three raw edges (sides and bottom) under ¼ inch, and press with an iron. Fold under ¼ inch again, and press. Using the needle and thread or a sewing machine, sew the hems with a running stitch (see page 10).

5 Sew the darts along the pins. Remove pins. Fold the waist under ¼ inch, and press. Fold under ¼ inch again, and press. Sew the waist hem.

6 Pin the ribbon to the outside of the waist, beginning at the edge of the inner flap and ending at the edge of the outside flap (see illustration). The ribbon should extend 12 inches from the outer flap of the skirt; trim off any excess. Sew the ribbon to the waist. Remove pins.

7 Sew a 12-inch length of ribbon to the waistband on the outside of the inside flap (see illustration).

8 If desired, decorate your skirt by sewing bead fringe, lace, ribbon, or a marabou boa along the bottom hemline. Or add a shorter, sheer panel to the skirt at step 2 as shown in the photo.

9 If necessary, sew a Velcro dot to the inside of the waistband to secure the inner flap to the outer flap.

Variation: This looks best with a long flowing skirt, but an abbreviated version will work on a short skirt. Sew at least 4 yards of ribbon around the waist and don't trim off the excess. Sew 3 yards of ribbon to the side of the waistband of the outer flap (see illustration). Then wrap the ribbons around your body in a crisscross pattern down your hips (not too tight!) and tie the ribbon in a bow 3 inches above your knees.

pippi longstocking SKIRT

Cool girl Pippi used whatever she had around—striped tights, big shoes, and a patchwork skirt. Snappy style without any effort, the way it should be. This everything-but-the-kitchen-sink mix can include rickrack, faux fur, and ball fringe, it's up to you!

1 Using a running stitch (see page 10), sew a row of trimming above the hem of the skirt. Repeat with more trimming if desired.

2 Sew a row of ribbon around the waist-band.

3 If desired, sew ball fringe along the hem. Then add a faux fur pocket!

Needle or a sewing machine
Thread to match the trimming
1 cotton skirt, plain or print
4 to 6 yards trimming, such as ribbon and rickrack
Optional: Faux fur and ball fringe.

pippi's out-on-the-town SKIRT

Even Pippi must dress up sometimes.

Tape measure
1 straight skirt, with a simple bold pattern
Scissors
Beaded or silk fringe (see step 1
   below to determine the length)
Pins
Needle or a sewing machine
Thread to match the ribbon
2 yards 1-inch-wide ribbon
Sequin ribbon
Sequins
Beads

1 Using the tape measure, determine the circumference of the skirt's hem. Using scissors, cut the fringe to the measurement. Pin in place. Using the needle and thread or a sewing machine, sew the fringe to the hem with a running or hemming stitch (see pages 10 and 11).

2 Using a running stitch or whipstitch (see page 10), sew a ribbon to cover the fringe stitches.

3 Sew the sequin ribbon on the skirt, following the printed pattern of the fabric.

4 Dot sequins across the pattern. Attach each sequin individually, securing it with a bead in the center (see page 13).

quick skirt or DRESS OVERHAUL

Everyone has a closet full of boring going-to-work clothes, usually in black, gray, and brown wool. But going to work doesn't have to be so depressing. Add a zing to your shift with a small detail.

Embroidery needle
1 skein embroidery thread, in hot pink, acid green, or yummy orange
1 drab skirt or dress
Four 12-inch-long strands of seed beads, in silver or a dark color
Scissors
Multipurpose cement glue
Needle
Thread to match the beads

1 Using the embroidery needle and thread, sew a simple running stitch (or a fancier stitch; see pages 10–11) in a line 2 inches above, and all the way around, the hem of the skirt or dress.

2 If you're feeling revolutionary, add strands of seed beads to the hem. If your seed bead strands are in loops, using scissors, cut the loop at the knot. Tie off both ends and seal each knot with a drop of multipurpose cement glue. Let the glue dry. Using the needle and thread, sew a stitch every inch, letting a 1½-inch length of beads dangle between each stitch (see page 13).

Variation: Cut the hem off the skirt and fray the raw edge by unraveling ½ inch of the threads along the hem, creating a fringe of fabric (à la Chanel). Using a running stitch, sew a ribbon in a line just above the frayed edge to prevent further fraying. Add the embroidery detail above the ribbon.

another quick CHANGE

An easy-to-add panel of color gives a fresh kick to an old skirt.

Tape measure
1 bland skirt or dress
Scissors
½ yard colorful sheer or silk fabric
Iron
Needle or a sewing machine
Thread to match the sheer fabric, skirt, and ribbon
Pins
1 to 2 yards ribbon
Optional: Sequin ribbon

1 Using the tape measure, determine the circumference of the skirt's hem. Using scissors, cut a piece of fabric 3 to 6 inches wide and the length of the circumference of the hem (you may have to join together a few pieces of fabric to equal this measurement). Fold one long side of the fabric under ¼ inch, and press with the iron. Fold under ¼ inch again, and press. Using needle and thread or a sewing machine, sew the hem with a running stitch (see page 10) along the length.

2 Pin the raw edge of the fabric to the outside of the hem of the skirt. Sew the fabric to the hem. Remove pins.

3 Using a running stitch or whipstitch (see page 10), sew the ribbon in place, covering the raw edge of the fabric.

4 If desired, sew a line of sequin ribbon along the top or bottom edge of the ribbon.

spin-around circle SKIRT

Although we ought to run from most theme clothing (the sweatshirt with puffy-paint teddy bears being the most obvious example), there is nothing wrong with revisiting the good old, decorated-felt circle skirt. You needn't stick to decorating it with poodles on rhinestone leashes, either. How about one trimmed with martini glasses to wear to a cocktail party at your bachelorette pad? Or scenes of Venice for an Italian bon voyage party?

Scissors
2 to 4 squares of 9-inch-by-12-inch felt, in the color(s) of your choice
Needle
Thread to match felt
Sequins
Beads
1 full cotton skirt

1 Using scissors, cut out shapes from the felt (approximately 4 inches by 4 inches is a good size).

2 Using needle and thread, sew sequins on the cutouts, attaching each sequin individually and securing it with a bead in the center (see page 13).

3 Using a tiny whipstitch (see page 10) around the edges of the cutouts, sew the cutouts in place around the bottom half of your skirt.

Variation: Use fusible interfacing and an iron to attach the cutouts to the skirt. Then use fabric glue to attach the sequins to the felt quickly and easily. It won't be as permanent, but you'll be dressed a whole lot faster.

swan lake ballerina SKIRT

This dreamy skirt is perfect for sashaying around the house and pretending your name is Giselle. If you're practical (don't make a habit of it!), try wearing it over a long, slim silk skirt. Netting is fabulous because it needn't be hemmed, and it's cheap, cheap, cheap.

Tape measure
Scissors
3 yards 1-inch-wide ribbon
Pins
2 to 4 yards tulle (amount depends on the desired fullness of the skirt)
Needle or a sewing machine
Thread to match ribbon

1 Using a tape measure, determine the circumference of your waist. Using scissors, cut a length of ribbon to that measurement.

2 Pin your fabric to this ribbon, gathering the tulle fabric as you go. The more you gather, the fuller your skirt will be. Using the needle and thread or a sewing machine, sew the gathered tulle to the ribbon with a running stitch (see page 10) down the middle of the ribbon. Remove pins.

3 Trim the skirt to the length you want.

4 Pin the remaining ribbon over the raw side of the tulle along the waist, leaving an equal amount of loose ribbon on each end of the skirt waist, like an apron. Using a whipstitch (see page 10), sew the top edge of this ribbon to the top edge of the first ribbon. Then sew the bottom edge of the ribbon to the fabric. Remove pins.

5 Tie the ribbon around your waist and practice your pirouettes.

simple slip DRESS

You can make this dress from floaty fabric, soft silk, or see-through organza. Make two or three, and try layering a diaphanous one over a sparkly one. Start with the basic garment, then select one of the variations for the finishing details.

Tape measure
Scissors
2 to 4 yards fabric
Needle or a sewing machine
Thread to match the fabric
Iron
1 yard silk cord

1 Using a tape measure, determine the circumference of the widest part of your body; add an additional 4 inches to this measurement. Using scissors, cut fabric according to this measurement for the width and to the length you desire—short and sweet or long and luxurious. Determine the length measurement, starting 3 inches below your collar bone and proceeding down to your knees or your ankles.

2 Using the needle and thread or a sewing machine, sew the two side edges of the fabric together, right sides facing, with a running stitch (see page 10). This will create a fabric tube.

3 Fold the bottom edge under ¼ inch, and press with the iron. Fold under ¼ inch again, and press. Using a running or a hemming stitch (see pages 10 and 11), sew the bottom hem in place.

4 Fold the top edge under ¼ inch, and press. Fold under ¼ inch again, and press. Using a running stitch, sew the top hem in place.

5 Using the tape measure, determine the length of one of your bra straps; add an additional 2 inches to this measurement. Using scissors, cut two

(continued)

pieces of silk cord, each to this measurement. Using a running stitch, sew the silk cord straps in place along the top edge.

Variation 1: Just below the bustline, sew one end of a 6-inch length of ribbon 1 inch in from one of the side seams. Repeat on the other side with another 6-inch length of ribbon. Tie the ribbon while wearing the dress, for a fitted shape. If you wish, attach longer ribbons to wrap around your body a few times before tying.

Sew little flowers and beads along the straps and neckline.

Variation 2: Using scissors, cut a piece of fabric that is 1 inch wide and as long as your width measurement from step 1.

Fold the raw edges under ¼ inch, and press with an iron.

Turn the dress inside out. Pin the fabric to the inside of the dress just below the bustline. Using a needle and thread or a sewing machine, sew the fabric to the dress with a running stitch along each edge. This will create a channel for a ribbon tie.

Turn the dress right side out. Make a tiny slit in the outside center front of the channel. Using a whipstitch (see page 10), bind the edges of the slit. Attach a safety pin to one end of a ribbon. Using the safety pin as a guide, thread the ribbon into the slit, through the channel, and out again. Pull the ribbon to gather the garment, and tie for a fitted shape.

Using a running stitch, sew four or five stitches in a vertical line down the center front of the bodice (beginning at the neckline and then down a few inches). The last stitch should end with the needle and thread on the inside of the dress. Pull the ends of the thread to gather the fabric, creating a V neck. Knot the threads.

Finish by sewing bead-embroidered ribbon along the neckline.

wraps & cozies

Snuggle up in style. From airy gauze to fuzzy wool, a shawl around your shoulders is as comfy as a security blanket, and oh, so fashiony, too. Scarves and caps will keep your 'do under wraps!

Lucky Stars Fairy Shawl (page 74)

lucky stars fairy SHAWL

Bossing around Cobweb and Mustardseed, arguing with Oberon, and being harassed by Puck are just part of the busy routine of a royal fairy. At least you can look enchanting while at work in the woods, in this shimmering whisper of a wrap. The details flicker like fireflies in the midsummer moonlight. Look in the drapery section of the fabric store for just the right glimmering material.

2-foot-by-6-foot piece of translucent, opalescent fabric
Iron
Needle or a sewing machine
Thread to match the fabric
Clear fabric glue
6 feet of plastic wrap
Glittery fabric paint
Beads
Glitter
Optional: Embroidery thread, crystal beads

1 Fold the edges of the fabric under ¼ inch, and press with the iron. Fold under ¼ inch again, and press. Using the needle and thread or a sewing machine, sew the hem with a running stitch (see page 10). (Or carefully apply glue to the very edges to keep them from fraying.)

2 Place plastic wrap under the fabric. Using glittery fabric paint, create flowers, dragon-flies, and other ethereal images. If you need help with your artistic endeavor, you can place an image under the fabric for use as a guide. Let the paint dry.

3 Using a running stitch, sew beads along the painted designs (see page 13). Drip on swirls of glue and sprinkle with glitter. Let dry.

4 If desired, add fringe to the ends of the scarf. Using the embroidery needle, guide a 5-inch-long length of embroidery thread through the bottom edge of one of the short ends of your scarf. Knot the two ends of the embroidery thread together next to the fabric. Slip crystal beads onto strands of the fringe. Then knot the end of each strand individually so that the bead can slide up and down the strand. Repeat along both short ends of the shawl, beginning at one corner, spacing the strands every ½ inch, and ending at the opposite corner.

velvet vixen WRAP

Velvet is easy to emboss with simple images. The fabric can then be used as a luxurious wrap. Or use this same technique to create a one-of-a-kind fabric trim for skirts, jeans, or any other garments that need a little dose of extravagance.

Rubber stamps (use simple images with thick lines or create your own from kits available at craft- and art-supply stores)
Ironing board
2-foot-by-6-foot piece of synthetic velvet
Iron
Needle or a sewing machine
Thread to match the fabric
Optional: Tassels

1 Place a rubber stamp, image side up, on the ironing board. Cover the stamp with a section of velvet, fuzzy side down.

2 Place the iron, on a medium-hot setting, on the velvet for a few seconds. Do not move the iron back and forth. Carefully remove the iron and check to see if the velvet is embossed yet. (Since each iron is different, you may need to experiment with heat settings and time lengths. Just don't set the house on fire! Begin with a lower setting and a shorter amount of time and go up from there.)

3 Repeat the pattern all over the entire fabric or just create a border.

4 To finish the wrap, fold the edges under ¼ inch, and press. Fold over ¼ inch again, and press. Using the needle and thread or a sewing machine, sew the hem with a running stitch (see page 10).

5 If you desire, sew tassels along the two short ends.

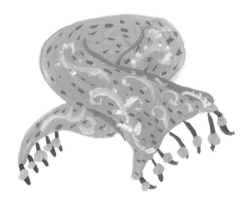

babylon BOA

Find an old, sheer scarf—the kind that women used to control their beehives. Add a few exotic details for a hot, hot curry look. Visit the local Indian import shop for bindi dots and stock up on vindaloo sauce while you're there!

Needle
Thread to match the scarf
100 mermaid scales
1 sheer scarf
Embroidery needle
1 skein embroidery thread
30 *bindi* dots

1 Using the needle and thread, sew the mermaid scales, evenly spaced, along the edges of the scarf (see page 14).

2 Using the embroidery needle and thread, sew a decorative running stitch (see page 10) around the perimeter.

3 Dot the *bindis* across the scarf and secure in place with a few stitches.

sequin flower SCARF

An enchanted garden to wrap around your neck on chilly, daydreaming strolls. Revamp an old woolen scarf or look for soft knit yardage at the fabric store.

1-foot-by-5-foot piece of soft wool
Iron
Needle or a sewing machine
Thread to match fabric
50 sequin flowers (available ready-made from craft-supply stores)
Embroidery needle
Leaf-green embroidery thread (or in a color to match the flowers)
Optional: Tailor's chalk

1 Fold the edges of the fabric under ¼ inch, and press with the iron. Fold under ¼ inch again, and press. Using a needle and thread or a sewing machine, sew each hem with a running or hemming stitch (see page 11).

2 Scatter the sequin flowers around the scarf. Sew each in place individually.

3 Using the embroidery needle and embroidery thread, stitch stems and little leaves around the flowers. If you need a guide, mark flowing lines with tailor's chalk.

french picnic SCARF

Create that je-ne-sais-quoi look. A sweet little head scarf is trés bien!

Tape measure
Pencil
Straightedge
Craft paper
Scissors
Pins
17-inch-by-17-inch piece of fabric
Iron
Needle or a sewing machine
Thread to match fabric
1 yard ½-inch-wide ribbon or seam binding
Optional: Flower patch

1 Using a tape measure, measure from the middle of one ear up over the top of your head and down to the middle of your other ear.

2 Using the pencil and the straightedge, draw a line on the craft paper as long as this measurement. From the center point of that line, draw a perpendicular line, 9 inches long. Connect the ends of the lines to form a triangle (see illustration).

3 Using scissors, cut out the paper pattern, and pin it to the fabric. Cut the triangle shape out of the fabric. Remove the pins and the pattern.

4 Fold all the edges under ¼ inch, and press. Fold under ¼ inch again, and press. Using the needle and thread or a sewing machine, sew the hem on each side with a running stitch (see page 10).

5 Sew the ribbon or seam binding to the long edge of the triangle. Be sure to leave enough ribbon on the ends to tie at the back of your neck. If you like, add a flower patch to the tip of the scarf.

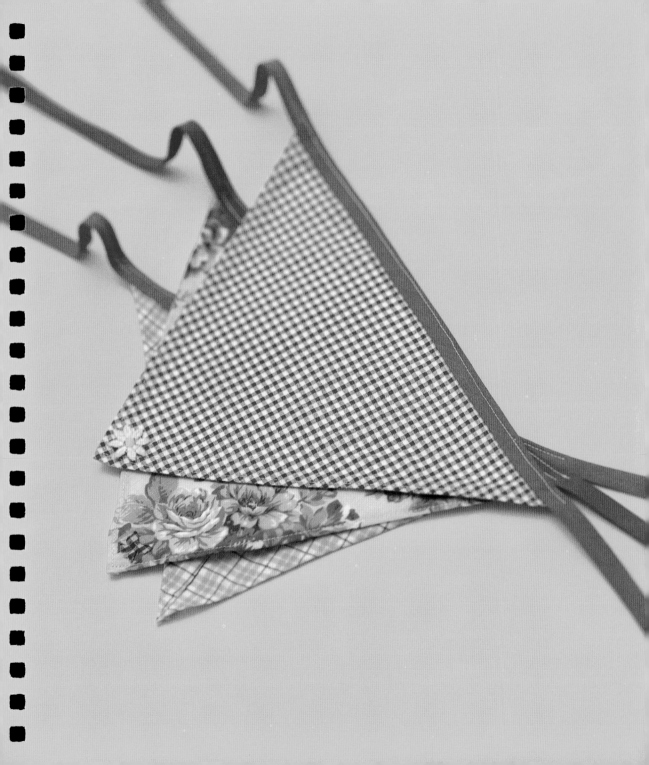

the perfect PONCHO

Just as simple to make as the cut-a-hole-and-stick-your-head-through style but so, so chic. You won't believe you're that stylish. Use blanket material or thick, wool felt for the warmest wrap.

2½ yards wool felt or blanket fabric
Scissors
Large-eyed needle
Yarn
Needle
Thread to match the fabric
1 cool button (perhaps big Bakelite button)

1 Wrap the material just on the outside edge of your shoulders. Using scissors, trim the fabric so that the two top corners just overlap in front (see illustration).

2 Using the large-eyed needle and yarn, bind all the edges using a folk-art stitch (see page 11) .

3 Cut a buttonhole in the corner of the upper edge. Using yarn, bind the hole with a whipstitch (see page 10).

4 Using the needle and thread, sew the button to the opposite corner.

warm wooly CAP

When the winter winds blow, opt for this goofy-in-a-good-way cap.

1 stocking cap
Craft paper
Pencil
Scissors
Knitted or fleece fabric, or an old sweater
Embroidery needle
1 skein embroidery thread, or yarn

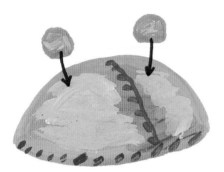

1 Place the stocking cap flat on the craft paper and, with the pencil, trace the outline.

2 Using scissors, cut out the paper pattern, and pin it to the fabric. Cut the pattern shape out of the fabric. Repeat so you have two sides for your cap.

3 Using the embroidery needle and thread or yarn, sew the two sides together with a decorative folk-art stitch (see page 11). Continue along all the outside edges.

4 If you like, cut ear shapes out of the fabric. Finish the edges with a folk-art stitch and sew them in place on the top of the cap.

heavenly handbags

There was a time when the handbag had to match the shoes and the hat and the gloves. Be happy those days are dead and gone! Celebrate by creating a kooky handbag that's as outrageous as the rest of your outfit.

Movie Star Handbag (page 89)

easy drawstring evening BAG

When just one bright-red lip-stick is all you need, take along this simple little bag to swing from your wrist. Create it from some fantastic fabric: fiery-red dragon-print silk, mirrored and embroidered Indian textiles, or kilim-style weaves.

Pencil
Craft paper
Scissors
Pins
½ yard printed silk, embroidered
    textiles, or kilim-style fabric
Needle
Thread
½ yard velvet
Safety pin
1 yard velvet cord

1 Take a saucer or another round object of a similar size (approximately 6 inches in diameter) and, using the pencil, trace it onto the craft paper. Using scissors, cut the circle pattern out of the paper.

2 Pin the pattern to the fabric and cut the circle shape out of the fabric.

3 Next, you'll need to determine the circle's perimeter (the distance around the out-side edge). Does everyone remember this formula from geometry class? The perimeter is the diameter multiplied by 3.14 (our friend pi). For example, a circle with a 6-inch diameter has an 18.84-inch perimeter (6 x 3.14). Ugh! And you thought sewing was exhausting. Now cut a rectangle of fabric that is 8 inches wide and as long as the perimeter plus 1 inch.

4 Fold the fabric in half, right sides facing, to form an 8-inch-by-9.42-inch rectangle, for example, if the perimeter measure-ment is 18.84. Using needle and thread, sew a seam ½ inch from the edge along the 8-inch side of the rectangle with a running stitch (see page 10).

5 Open the fabric into a tube shape. Pin the fabric circle to one end, right sides facing (see illustra-tion). Sew a seam around the base.

6 Repeat steps 1 through 5 using the velvet fabric, to create the lining.

7 Turn the outer fabric right side out. Leave the lining material wrong-side out and insert the lining material into the opening on the outer fabric. Line up the side seams of the two fabrics. Pin together along the top edge to keep the two layers even. Sew through both layers 3 inches down from the top, all the way around, and then again 2½ inches down from the top. This is the channel for the velvet cord.

8 Fold the raw edge of each fabric under ¼ inch around the top edge, and pin together. Sew the two layers of fabric together.

9 Make a ¼-inch vertical slit through the outer layer of the channel at the seam. Using a whipstitch (see page 10), bind the edges of the slit.

10 Attach the safety pin to one end of the velvet cord and, using the safety pin as a guide, thread the cord through the slit, around the channel, and out again. Knot the ends of the cord together and cinch the top closed. Leave the cord long to go over your shoulder, or shorten it for wearing on your wrist.

happy cherry felt PURSE

Oh joy! A giggly paperbag-style purse made from colorful felt. Decorate it with felt cherries, flowers, animals, or anything that makes you hum a la-la tune.

Scissors
Three 9-inch-by-9-inch squares of
   felt (all the same color)
Pinking shears
Embroidery needle
Embroidery thread
12-inch-long ribbon
Pins
Scrap felt (in various colors)
Optional: Sequins, beads

1 Using scissors, cut one square of felt, vertically, into three equal sections.

2 Using pinking shears, cut a zigzag edge along one side of each square and along one end of two of the narrow strips. Leave one narrow strip without zigzag detail.

3 Using the needle and embroidery thread, attach the pieces together with a decorative folk-art stitch (see page 11), so that the zigzag pattern is continuous along the top (see illustration). The plain strip forms the bottom.

4 Cut the ribbon into two equal lengths. The two ribbon strips will be the handles.

5 Form one ribbon into an arch at the center top of one side. Pin the handle in place on the inside. Attach the handle by stitching a criss-cross pattern on the ends. Repeat on the other side.

6 Create felt cutout decorations (see page 14). Using a whipstitch (see page 10), sew them on the sides of the purse.

7 If you like, add sequin to the decorations, sewing a bead through the center of each sequin.

Variation: Add to or replace the felt cutouts with kid-style embroidery. Embroider names, wispy flowers, or silly animals onto your purse. Using tailor's chalk, make a quick sketch of the desired shapes on the purse. Using embroidery thread, stitch along the chalklines with a running stitch or try a fancier stitch (see pages 10–11).

movie star HANDBAG

Even if you're just waiting to be discovered, you can still look like Zsa-Zsa, dah-ling! This ultra-glamorous handbag can be trimmed with boa, for dramatic divas.

Scissors
½ yard glamorous sequin fabric, silver lamé, or faux zebra fur
½ yard satin
Needle
Thread to match the glamorous fabric
Pins
12-inch-long ribbon or 2 rhinestone kitty collars
Optional: Marabou boa, tassels

1 Using scissors, cut both pieces of fabric according to the illustration.

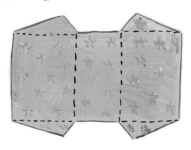

2 Using a needle and thread, sew along the sides (right sides facing) and then along the base of the exterior fabric (see illustration).

3 Repeat with the satin lining fabric.

4 Turn the exterior fabric right side out and fit the satin lining into the top opening. Fold the raw edges of each under ¼ inch and pin them together to secure. Using scissors, cut the ribbon in half or unbuckle the kitty collars and cut off the buckles. Form a loop handle by inserting the ends of one ribbon or collar between the two fabrics on one side (see illustration). Pin in place. Repeat on the other side.

5 Sew the two layers of fabric together along the top edge.

6 If desired, sew the marabou boa trim over the top edge seam, adding a tassel every few inches, or in the center.

sunny summer BAG

Find a wacky straw souvenir tote at the thrift store, trim it with fabric flowers, and make it as happy as a bumblebee.

Scissors
4 yards grosgrain ribbon
Needle
Thread to match the ribbon
1 straw bag (about 6 by 8 inches)
Fabric Flowers

1 Using scissors, cut the length of grosgrain ribbon in half.

2 Using a needle and thread, stitch one end of the grosgrain ribbon to the base of one of the handles. Wrap the ribbon around the handle, securing the end of the ribbon with a stitch at the opposite end of the handle.

3 Repeat the same steps on other handle.

4 Sew fabric flowers onto the surface of the bag as desired.

big plastic PURSE

A sturdy bag to control even the most out-of-control piles of junk. Your favorite images decorate the sides. You'll need to visit a copy shop for this project.

Glue stick
Color copies of your favorite copyright-free
   images, enough to cover all the sheets of
   construction paper
Two 8½-inch-by-11-inch sheets of
   construction paper

Two 6-inch-by-11-inch sheets
   of construction paper
One 6-inch-by-8½-inch sheet of
   construction paper
Thimble
Embroidery needle
1 to 2 skeins embroidery thread
Hole punch
1½ feet ball chain (the kind used for
   key chains)

1 Using the glue stick, attach the color copy images to one side of each construction paper sheet. Have the sheets laminated at a copy shop with medium-thick laminate.

2 Don your thimble! Using the embroidery needle, pierce holes 1 inch apart along the long edges and one short edge of each 8½-inch-by-11-inch piece and each 6-inch-by-11-inch piece. Make holes on all sides of the 6-inch-by-8½-inch piece.

3 Assemble the pieces into a box shape, so that the 6-inch-by-8½-inch piece is on the bottom, and the top is open (the images should be on the outside). Using the needle and embroidery thread, sew the sides together using a loose whipstitch through the pierced holes (see illustration and page 10).

4 Sew in the bottom panel.

5 Using the hole punch, make two holes for the handle, 4 inches apart and 1 inch from the top, on one 8½-inch-by-11-inch side panel. Repeat on the other side.

6 Cut the chain into two equal lengths. To create handles, thread chain through the holes on one side. Secure the chain to itself in a loop with the keychain-style attachment. Repeat on the other side.

miss mermaid BIKINIPACK

The loveliest of the sea stows her bikini top in this simple sling pack made from an old T-shirt. So what if she smells a bit fishy!

Scissors
1 T-shirt (vintage iron-on, a favorite surf tee, or striped)
Needle

Thread to match the T-shirt and ribbon
Iron
1½ yards web strapping or rock-climbing rope
Pins
1 yard decorative fabric ribbon
Embroidery needle
1 skein embroidery thread
7-inch-by-5-inch sheet of clear vinyl

1 Using scissors, cut the sleeves and the neck off the T-shirt. Cut a straight vertical line from the top of the seam below the sleeve to the top of the shoulder, then cut a straight horizontal line under the neck. Cut through both layers of fabric (the front and the back) at once.

2 Turn the tee inside out. Using a needle and thread, sew a vertical seam up each side with a running stitch (see page 10).

3 Turn right side out. Fold the top edge of the tee under 1 inch, and press with an iron. Fold under 1 inch again and press. Sew an inset seam (see page 12) along the fold, almost 1 inch from the outer edge. This will create a channel for the strap.

4 Cut a small vertical slit in the center back of the channel. Thread the strap into the slit, through the channel, and

out again. Pull on the ends until they are even with each other.

5 Tuck each end of the strap into the corresponding bottom corner of the tee. Pin in place. Turn the tee inside out. Sew a seam along the bottom, joining the back and front panels together, and stitching through the straps. Turn the tee right side out.

6 Sew two horizontal rows of decorative ribbon to the front of the pack, one 2 inches above the bottom and another 2 inches below the top.

7 Using the embroidery needle and embroidery thread, sew the clear vinyl rectangle to the lower ⅓ of the front with a running stitch. Sew along the two sides and the bottom of the vinyl to form a pocket.

fun TOTE

Use colorful fabrics and your favorite photo to create this fanciful tote.

Needle or a sewing machine
Thread
4-inch-by-24-inch piece of fabric
12-inch-by-24-inch piece of fabric

1½-inch-by-24-inch piece of fabric
Pins
Scissors
20 inches ribbon
14 inches sequin ribbon
3-inch-by-4-inch plastic photo sleeve
A favorite photo or image
Optional: Embroidered patches

1 Using the needle and thread or a sewing machine, sew the 4-inch-by-24-inch strip of fabric to the bottom 4 inches of the 12-inch-by-24-inch fabric with a running stitch (see page 10 and illustration).

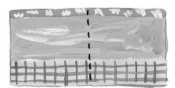

2 Using a running stitch, sew the 1½-inch-by-24-inch strip of fabric to the top 1½ inches of the 12-inch-by-24-inch fabric.

3 Fold the 12-inch-by-24-inch fabric piece in half, right sides facing, to form a 12-inch-by-12-inch square. Using a running stitch, sew a seam along the side opposite the fold and across the bottom. Fold the top edge over ¼ inch, pin, and sew in place. Turn the tote right side out.

4 Using scissors, cut the ribbon into two equal lengths. Pin the ribbon to the inside top of the opening, forming loop handles. Sew in place.

5 Sew the sequin ribbon around the edge of the photo sleeve. Sew only through the top layer of the sleeve so that the photo will still be able to slide inside.

6 Sew the sequined sleeve to the center front of the tote with a running stitch. Sew along the two sides and the bottom of the photo sleeve to form a pocket.

7 Insert the photo into the photo sleeve.

8 If desired, decorate the sides by sewing the embroidered patches in place.

hair doodads & oddball accessories

All the odds and ends to complete your outré outfit.

Oh-So-Rosy Bobby Pins (page 98)

oh-so-rosy BOBBY PINS

Cultivate a flower garden in your coif.

12 regular bobby pins
1 sheet of paper
Sparkly green nail polish
12 tiny silk rosebuds with wire stems

1 Clip a bobby pin to a sheet of paper. Paint the top of the bobby pin with the nail polish. Let dry.

2 Wrap the stem of a rosebud around and around the top of the bobby pin. Trim off any excess stem.

Variation: Use fabric daisies instead of rosebuds. Glue flat-backed plastic jewels on the petals of the daisy. Then poke a length of florist's wire through the center of the daisy. Wrap the wire around the top of the bobby pin.

rhinestone CHOKER

*Make a few sparkly chokers
using various colors and sizes
of ribbons and jewels.*

Tailor's chalk
Ruler
1 yard velvet ribbon
Rhinestone-attachment tool
12 to 24 rhinestones
Scissors

1 Using tailor's chalk and a ruler, make
evenly spaced dots along the center of
the velvet ribbon (see illustration).

2 Using the rhinestone-attachment tool,
attach the rhinestones onto the dots.

3 Tie the ribbon around your neck and,
using scissors, trim off the excess ribbon.

hollywood hair CLIPS

Dazzling, old clip-on earrings are a Princess Charming must have, but they hurt like heck and weigh at least 200 pounds apiece. Instead, attach them to hair clips for painless sparkle.

1 pair jeweled clip-on earrings
2 metal barrettes
Multipurpose cement glue or unwaxed dental floss

1 Unscrew, break off, or otherwise get rid of the clip on the back of each earring.

2 Attach the earring to the barrette: The design of your earring will dictate the method of attachment. Earrings that have an open pattern or clusters of jewels with space in between should be tied. Using dental floss, loop the floss through the jewels and around the barrette two to three times. Tie a knot behind the barrette and seal with a drop of multipurpose cement glue.

Flat-backed, closed-design earrings should be glued. Using glue, attach the earring to the top of the barrette. Repeat on the other earring.

Variation: Use fabric flowers instead of earrings.

kitty princess TIARA

*Princess of your domain?
Not without a tiara! This
tiara will make you a real
pussycat princess, and don't
let some dumb boy tell you
otherwise. Let heads roll!*

Plain metal or plastic
  headband (optional)
Four 12-inch-long
  metallic pipe
  cleaners
Scissors
Multipurpose
  cement glue
Rhinestones, other
  mini-jewels, and fake flowers

1 Start with a plain headband, or make your own by wrapping one of the pipe cleaners over the top of your head.

2 Using a pipe cleaner, create three even loops. Attach each loop to the center of the headband by wrapping it tightly or gluing around the band (see illustration).

3 Use another pipe cleaner to make two loops on top of the three loops. Using scissors, trim off excess pipe cleaner. Use the excess to make one more loop above the two loops, forming the top (see illustration).

4 Glue rhinestones, jewels, and fake flowers to the pipe cleaners. Let the glue dry.

starlet SLIDES

Cheap, clear Lucite heels can be dressed up with removable toe trim. Choose different looks for the red carpet, the dressing room, or "doing" lunch.

Sandpaper

1 pair clear Lucite heels (if you can't find these in a trashy lingerie catalog just use flip-flops)

Velcro dots

Multipurpose cement glue

Unwaxed dental floss

Needle

Thimble

Fur pom-poms, marabou boa, fake flowers, old clip-on jeweled earrings, and/or plastic toys

1 Using sandpaper, sand a coin-sized area in the center of the toe strap on each shoe.

2 Take the fuzzy side of a Velcro dot and glue it to the roughened spot. (Although many Velcro dots are self-adhesive, they still need help. If they insist on falling off, show them who's boss and make a stitch in the center with dental floss and a large needle. Don a thimble first to keep your fingers safe.)

3 Using multipurpose cement glue or needle and dental floss, attach the rough sides of the Velcro dots to an assortment of trimmings.

4 Attach trimming to fuzzy Velcro on each shoe, and change your toe décor according to your mood.

 gigi FLATS

The final touch for your French picnic fantasy. The minxy ribbon lacing is so comfy it won't cramp your joie de vivre.

Scissors
2 yards ½-inch-wide ribbon (or ¹⁄₁₆-inch-wide for a strappy look)
Needle
Thread
1 pair pink or black ballet slippers
1-foot-by-1-foot square of ¹⁄₁₆-inch-thick rubber matting
Metallic marker
Clear upholstery adhesive (available at auto supply stores)

1 Using scissors, cut the ribbon into four 18-inch lengths.

2 Using needle and thread, sew the end of one ribbon to the inside of one slipper with a running stitch (see page 10), 3 inches from the back of the heel. Repeat on the other side. Repeat on the other slipper.

3 Place one slipper on the rubber matting and trace the outline with the metallic marker. Repeat with the other slipper. Cut the shapes, ¼ inch inset from the outline, from the matting.

4 Spread the upholstery adhesive evenly over the rubber pieces. Stick the shoe soles on to the rubber slipper shapes. Let dry.

fifties housewife APRON

You may be hard pressed to find a housewife among your acquaintances. But these delicious aprons make cooking look so fun and stylish that it's almost tempting. You can at least look great ordering takeout.

1 vintage hankie, embroidered tea towel, or piece of fabric (an 18-by-18-inch square)
1 yard ribbon or seam binding
Needle or sewing machine
Thread
Scissors
1 yard rickrack
1 yard eyelet lace
4-inch-by 4-inch piece of fabric
Iron

1 Center the top edge of the hankie along the ribbon. Using the needle and thread or a sewing machine, sew the ribbon to the hankie with a running stitch (see page 10). As you go along, make a gather here and there by folding a total of about ½ inch of hankie into your stitch.

2 Using scissors, cut a 4-inch length of rickrack and eyelet lace. Sew a line of rickrack inset 1 inch from one edge, and eyelet lace to the top edge, of the 4-inch-by-4-inch fabric. This is the apron pocket.

3 Fold the three raw edges (the edge without the eyelet lace) of the pocket under ¼ inch, and press with the iron. Sew the pocket to the front of the apron, lace-trimmed edge up.

4 Sew a line of rickrack 1 inch above the bottom hem of the apron. Then sew eyelet lace trim to the bottom hem. Now you're cooking!

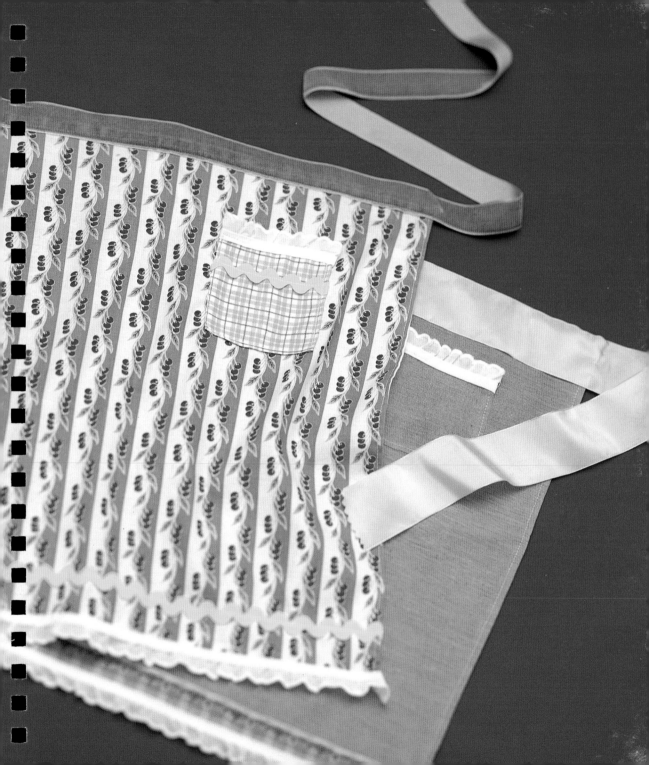

MATERIALS

✳ *fabric*

Fabric stores are full of lush velvets and silks, soft wools and fleeces, sugary florals and ginghams, shiny vinyls and plastics, wild and tame faux fur, and glittering draperies and retro reproductions—be sure to look at everything. Serious visits to a few stores are necessary. Just like clothing stores, there are huge marts with thousands of choices, as well as little boutiques full of heavenly imports. Fabric can be very expensive, so don't be shocked by the prices. If you like, just buy a little for some trim for a tiny handbag.

But do not confine your material purchases to the fabric store. Think of the material gathering as the creative part of the project. Go to thrift stores to find fabrics, linens, tablecloths, hankies, fur, vintage patterns, and fun trimmings. Look for funky flowered aprons, bachelor-pad boomerang draperies, mod sixties print scarves, and slippery seventies polyester shirts. Also, look for classic items that can be adorned, such as plain cardigans and simple skirts. And you needn't look just in the sewing section. Look for old clothes in interesting fabrics that can be cut up without any guilt; visit the linens and toy sections too. Would an old afghan make a good poncho? Would a fruit-print vinyl tablecloth make a cute bag or a fun skirt? The answer is yes!

✳ *trim*

The most important part of adornment! Look for basic ribbons in a variety of materials—velvet, grosgrain, satin, even embroidered with flowers and hearts, ball fringe and beaded fringe, rickrack and flower-chain trim, innocent white eyelet and racy black lace, patches and miniature flowers, seed beads and buttons. Look for ready-made beaded and sequined shapes (if used thoughtfully you won't look like a vivacious grandma headed to a casino). All these items are available at most well-stocked fabric stores.

Also seek out costumey items such as loose sequins, sequin ribbon and fabric, faux furs, marabou boas, feathers, pom-poms, mermaid scales, and rhinestones. And don't forget other decorations, such as charms and milagros, mirrored disks, bead strands and bracelets, plastic flowers and fruit, costume jewelry, jiggly eyeballs, glitter, and *bindi* dots.

TOOLS

A few simple tools can make all your projects a breeze.

* *sewing machine*

Look for a nice, inexpensive but sturdy machine. Although buying a sewing machine may seem like a big step, it is worth it even if you only use it occasionally. Grandma might even have one hiding away somewhere.

* *needles*

Having a bunch of needles in different sizes, from slim beading needles to large embroidery needles, can make sewing a snap.

* *thread*

You'll want to keep on hand a selection of threads in basic and offbeat colors. Always have a few candy-colored skeins of embroidery thread around, too.

* *iron*

An iron is perfect for pressing fabric into shape before you sew, or afterwards to smooth out any puckers.

* *pins*

These hold things in place during sewing. Or you can use them to try out the fit or hem length before sewing.

* tape measure
The fastest way to a perfect fit.

* paper
Craft paper and brown package paper are sturdy and easy to use for making patterns. In a pinch try a paper bag!

* pinking shears
That zigzag cut is irresistible.

* scissors
Get a good, sharp pair that will last forever.

* tailor's chalk and washable fabric pen
These are great for making removable markings for seams and measurements.

* fabric glue
It's a must for quick fixes and simple projects.

* rhinestone-attachment tool
Who can resist twinkly, garish rhinestones? This tool will allow you to drench yourself in sparkles.

CLOTHING SOURCES

✳ *your closet*

And everybody else's too! This is the first place to look for items to adorn or cut up—abandoned jeans, denim jackets, boring cardigans, and strappy T-shirts are prime candidates. Help a lazy friend clean out her closet!

✳ *thrift stores*

Packed with old clothes, fabric, linens, and plenty of trim, thrifts are the place to find unique items and revampable clothing. Most communities have the biggies, Goodwill, Salvation Army, and St. Vincent de Paul. But seek out smaller shops sponsored by churches, humane societies, and senior centers. Look in the phone book under thrift stores, second-hand shops, and consignment shops.

✳ *vintage shops*

Even though they sell thrift store items at outrageous prices, you can sometimes find what you need in a hurry for a decent price.

✳ *garage sales and flea markets*

Browsing through junk is so much fun you wouldn't want to miss an opportunity!

✳ *import shops*

Look for gorgeous fabric and interesting trim. Head to the small ones downtown and avoid the megamarts. Chinese silks, mirrored Indian textiles, plastic Asian flip-flops, Mexican milagros, Guatemalan embroidery, and African beads are only the beginning.

✳ *internet*

The best-known of the Internet auction sites is eBay.com. It is similar to a vintage store—a place with lots of items but also a hot spot for collectors willing to pay anything for the right piece. There are deals to be found though, if you like the crazy atmosphere and last-minute bidding.

RESOURCES

Look in the library for books on sewing, embroidery, and beading for detailed instructions on techniques. While you're there check out some vintage fashion books, costume books, and bound copies of old magazines such as *Vogue* for ideas on color and style. Also, scour the thrifts for fun how-to-sew books. Or look in your local bookstore for these:

✳ *basic sewing and needlepoint*

101 Essential Tips: Basic Sewing by Chris Jefferys, DK Publishing

101 Needlepoint Stitches and How to Use Them by Hope Hanley, Dover Publishing

10-20-30 Minutes to Sew by Nancy Zieman, Oxmoor House

The Complete Book of Sewing by Deni Brown, Dorling Kindersley

✳ *beading*

Art of Seed Beading by Gourley, Davis, and Talbott, Sterling Publications

Beaded Tassels, Braids and Fringes by Valerie Campbell-Harding, Sterling Publications

Complete Beading for Beginners by Karen Rempel, Nightwood Editions

✳ *related subjects*

After a Fashion: How to Reproduce, Restore, and Wear Vintage Style by Frances Grimble, Lavolta Press

Cheap Date by Kira Jolliffe (editor), Slab O Concrete

Secondhand Chic by Christa Weil, Pocket Books

Thrift Score: The Stuff, The Method, The Madness by Al Hoff, Harper Perennial Library

Lulu *loves* to look her
laloveliest, help her try on
some ***Cheap Frills*** with a
quick ***snip snip.***

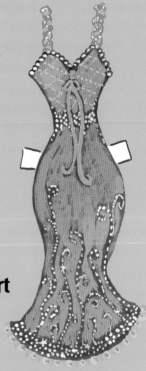

French Picnic Scarf

Simple Slip Dress

Happy Cherry Felt Purse

Heidi T-Shirt   ## Pippi's Out-on-the-Town Skirt

Fabulous Fur Cardigan

The Not-So-Basic Blue

Lulu LaLovely